© 2018 Ellis Potter

Without limiting the rights under copyright reserved above, no part of this publication may be reproduced, stored in, or introduced into a retrieval system, or transmitted in any form or by any means (electronic, mechanical, photocopying, or otherwise), without the prior written permission from the publisher, except where permitted by law, and except in the case of brief quotations embodied in critical articles and reviews. For information, write: info@destinee.ch

ISBN: 978-1-938367-41-0

Published by Destinée S.A. destineemedia.com
Editor Peco Gaskovski
Cover concept by Katherine Wolff
Cover and interior by Per Ole Lind
All rights reserved by the author.

THREE ELEMENTS

This book is made up of three elements – prose text, poetry and visual art. We can say these are the intellectual, the experiential and the visionary elements. In order to let these elements speak for themselves and support each other there are no elaborate comments included on the poem or the visual art. In receiving this book notice how the three elements comment on and complement each other.

Illustration for "The cloud of unknowing", **unknown artist**

BEFORE READING

For those readers who accept the religious assumption or presupposition that there is no supernatural part of reality, understanding this book will require a paradigm shift something like a color-blind person putting on glasses that allow them to see color. For those readers who already accept the religious assumption or presupposition that there is a supernatural part of reality, this book will give greater clarity and understanding to this belief.

– *E.H.P.*

DEDICATION

This book is dedicated to the people of the International English Speaking Church of Lausanne, who stimulated its writing by asking questions about my sermons.

Joshua passing the River Jordan with the Ark of the Covenant, Benjamin West (1738-1820)

1

INTRODUCTION

In the 14th Century two important books were written in the English language. One was the Canterbury Tales. The other one was The Cloud of Unknowing.

The Cloud of Unknowing is a book about how to get closer to God and experience Him. It was written by an English mystic. A mystic is a person who is aware of the supernatural dimensions of reality and has experiences of them. Most mystics think the supernatural dimensions are more real than the natural dimensions— that their visions and experiences are more real than baking bread or changing diapers. The author of The Cloud of Unknowing was most probably experiencing

Illustration for "The cloud of unknowing", unknown artist

what the Bible often calls the "Cloud": The Cloud of the Exodus and travelling in the desert, the Cloud of the Presence of God in the Tabernacle and Temple, the Cloud of Transfiguration, Ascension and Appearing. He or she evaluated and understood these experiences using Platonic and/or Gnostic assumptions and so concluded that to truly experience the supernatural one needs to forget, or "unknow", everything about the natural dimensions of reality. The Platonic and Gnostic worldviews assumed that reality is divided into a bottom half and a top half and we should choose the top half. Gnostic views can lead Christians to believe the bottom half, or creation, is totally bad and should be avoided so we can transcend and live in the top half with God, or that our spirits are saved and with God in the top half so it doesn't matter what we do here in the bottom half. The Bible is clear that there are supernatural dimensions but also clear that they are not more real than the natural ones. A main point of both Christmas and Easter is that they are physical, taking place in the natural dimensions. The Cloud the Bible talks about is an interface between the two. It helps us to know reality more completely. I will call it "The Cloud of Knowing".

The Cloud of Knowing is different from the Internet cloud because it is not virtual but real. It is not a place to keep things but an interface between the seen and the unseen worlds. It connects that part of reality that can be understood scientifically with that part which cannot.

Reality includes both the natural and supernatural dimensions, not just one or the other. Many students ask me, "What is Reality?" That's a fair question. Reality is who God is, what He does and what He wants. This includes you, of course, because God wants you to be, and wants you to be fully real. Anything that happens outside of who God is, what He does and what He wants is less than real because it is a distortion, unfounded variation or rebellion against the true reality. It is not stable or eternal and will vanish like a dream or a puff of smoke. Our suffering is not imaginary but it will not exist in eternity, and is not what God wants. Only that which is fully real or "Holy", and they who are fully real or "Holy", will remain forever.

Reality is divided into two parts in some ways. The first way is the division between the created reality and the uncreated reality. The uncreated reality consists of

God. This reality includes personality, language, relationships, dynamism, significance, choices, and more. The created reality consists of everything else and is also divided into two parts. The first part is space, time and energy, including rocks, trees and people, and is often referred to as the "natural" part. The second part is angels, both faithful and unfaithful, and energies and dimensions that science cannot measure; this part is often referred to as the "supernatural". Because this realty (both natural and supernatural) was created by the uncreated reality, it expresses its characteristics of personality, language, and so on. The created and uncreated parts of reality belong together.

The two parts of created reality are both similar and different. One similarity is that they are both dynamic and function in a matrix of sequence. A matrix is an atmosphere in which things happen. The matrix of tea is water. Tea happens in water. The matrix of sound is air. The matrix of email is cyberspace. The two parts of created reality are basically natural space and supernatural dimensions. The matrix of sequence (change, before and after, dynamism) in space is time. Things happen in time or they don't happen. The matrix of sequence outside of space is eternity. Eternity is not infinite time. It is a separate matrix, meaning that every point of time is present to every point of eternity. This fact can help us understand 2 Peter 3:8-9, which says "With the Lord a day is like a thousand years, and a thousand years are like a day." Eventually time and eternity will conflate and all that is real or holy will function in the unified matrix.

The Bible speaks of the Cloud in many places and sometimes calls it light, fire or darkness. The Cloud is an interface that allows people to be aware of the part of reality in the non-spatial dimensions. Because it connects people with unknown and unexperienced dimensions, those who experience it describe it in different ways. It is very difficult to describe non-spatial dimensions in language that normally describes spatial dimensions. People who experience the Cloud call it by various names, such as "burning bush", "pillar of fire or cloud", "blinding light", "angel", "chariot of fire" or "chariot throne", "flaming mountain", or "earthquake". The usual reaction to people who experience the Cloud is to fall down (sometimes as if dead), or kneel. Exposure to previously unexperienced parts of reality is a shock.

The Cloud is both a two-way street and a one-way street. Experiencing the revelatory and empowering Cloud is by invitation only. Those who find a way to break into the Cloud usually end up dead like Nadab and Abihu (Numbers 3:4). God often said to the Israelites "Don't come near" (without an invitation and preparation). The Cloud and the supernatural are not things we can just grab with the right technique. They are gifts, given to some presently and promised fully to everyone finally. Breaking into the Cloud is called "magic", "shamanism", "sorcery", or "witchcraft", all of which are forbidden in the Bible. God opens the Cloud sometimes for people and invites them to "draw near" or "come up here", and sustains them in the extraordinary experience. When people break into the Cloud they sometimes can't survive the experience.

Our way in the two-way street is basically prayer. When we say "Dear God" the interface opens up and we are speaking into eternity. We are always in the presence of the supernatural, God and eternity and are encouraged by the Bible to be aware of that all the time. The reality of the Cloud means God is always present for us. Prayer is like working in the same room with the Boss Who created the company. We can always talk to Him. While working we might forget He is there, but not for long. His presence is a stabilizing support and reference point for us. If we ignore the Boss and do sloppy, lazy or destructive work God will sustain the company (Kingdom) and we will be the losers.

The Cloud facilitates many things: prophecy, revelation, inspiration, visions, gifts, dreams, hearing God's Voice and more. In

April of 2015 as I approached my sixty-seventh birthday I began to think it might be time to travel less, slow down and write more. A few days later I heard a voice in my sleep. It was a masculine, calm, rather high-pitched voice, which said very clearly: "You have a good mind. Travel the world and help people to think." I woke up and sat up and said "OK." An interesting thing about this experience is that I was not listening for God's Voice. As I think about the many experiences of people in the Bible hearing God's voice it seems to me that none of them were listening either. It tends to come as a surprise.

Some people are more gifted or sensitive to the Cloud than others. People all through history and all over the world have experienced the Cloud and interpreted it in a great variety of ways. Many conclude from their experience that there is a supernatural reality and it is more real than the one we normally experience. They come to believe that the reality of space and time is an illusion and we need to transcend or unknow everything in order to be in a "higher" reality. They may develop techniques to achieve this transcendence. Often these experiences and techniques are therapeutic (relieving stress, helping to sleep and concentrate, making us feel connected) but they are not able to make us fully real. Only Jesus Christ can do that. Experiences of the supernatural cannot save us. The Bible is very clear that reality includes both the natural and supernatural. As mentioned earlier, Christmas and Easter are pointedly physical. The glorified resurrected body of Jesus was physical for forty days, touching, eating, discussing, working, being creative and practicing hospitality. His Body also functioned in the other dimensions, appearing and disappearing and "teleporting". It was completely real, not only supernatural.

Being aware of the Cloud can remind us that Truth cannot be reduced to fact but includes meaning or relationships. It cannot be reduced to the natural or supernatural parts of reality but includes both. It cannot be reduced to objectivity or subjectivity but includes both. The Truth of God is a full and living Truth.

2

THE CLOUD AND THE EARLY CHURCH

Many people in the early Church were Greeks. They came from a culture strongly shaped by the transcendentalism of Platonism and early Gnosticism, and so they naturally (not spiritually) brought this baggage with them into the Church. The Apostles did not buy into these tendencies, and almost all of the letters in the New Testament are fighting against the ideas of Platonism and Gnosticism. We see an example of this Apostolic fight in Colossians 2:18-19:

18. Do not let anyone who delights in false humility and the worship of angels disqualify you. Such a person also goes into

Moses and the burning bush, **Byzantine mosaic**

great detail about what they have seen; they are puffed up with idle notions by their unspiritual mind. 19. They have lost connection with the head, from whom the whole body, supported and held together by its ligaments and sinews, grows as God causes it to grow.

We see another example in 1 John 4:1-3:

1. Dear friends, do not believe every spirit, but test the spirits to see whether they are from God, because many false prophets have gone out into the world. 2. This is how you can recognize the Spirit of God: Every spirit that acknowledges that Jesus Christ has come in the flesh is from God, 3. but every spirit that does not acknowledge Jesus is not from God. This is the spirit of the antichrist, which you have heard is coming and even now is already in the world.

Both passages above are fighting for an understanding and practice of spirituality that is immanent and not only transcendent.

The prevalence of Platonism and early Gnosticism in the first generation of the Church is an example of a more general problem: the world is the salt and the light of the Church. This is not the way it was meant to be. In the Sermon on the Mount in Matthew 5:13-14, Jesus said: "You are the salt of the earth...You are the light of the world." This is what He said. This is what He meant. This is what He wants. However, He often doesn't get what He wants in the Church. Instead, the thoughts and values of various cultures of the world are constantly coming into the Church.

So, the Apostles seem to have lost the fight because Platonism, Gnosticism and other worldly ideas were not driven out of the Church. They have remained in the Church in every generation including our own. The fight goes on.

3

FAERIES, ELVES, WEE PEOPLE, TROLLS, ETC.

Accounts of supernatural creatures in the world's cultural history are so general they probably have some basis in supernatural fact. Children seem to be more aware of the Cloud or interface than adults. This is probably because their space-time model of reality has not become "solid" or "fixed" yet. It is not because they are innocent. If children can connect with parts of reality in or through the Cloud, they are also capable of making up creatures and/or what they say to manipulate grownups. Accounts of encounters with supernatural creatures have become so artistically and culturally distorted as to give very little useful

"Legend of the Sea"

information, only a true hint. Most of the stories I've heard or read show the role of the human person as initially passive. The supernatural approaches them or they stumble upon it. They don't go looking for it or figure it out. We should no more have a faerie hunt than a witch hunt.

Many people have a strong interest in contacting the dead in the supernatural. This is not a good idea and the Bible forbids it. Just because someone is dead doesn't mean they are wiser, friendlier or more honest than they were before. The witch at Endor had the capacity to contact the dead but she and everyone else knew she was wrong to do it. We must not reach into the supernatural to get power or wisdom. The supernatural contains both good and evil. That is why the Lord's Prayer includes "deliver us from evil". We must test the spirits to see if they know that Jesus Christ has come in the flesh and not naively believe something just because it is supernatural.

Not only folk tales come from Cloud encounters, but religions as well. A Religion is a way of reconnecting with a disconnected reality—that is, to "re-ligament" or tie back (related to the Latin word religare). Religions result from people experiencing something of the supernatural and building a system to reconnect. Christianity is not a religion but the opposite. Christianity is not a matter of people discovering other aspects of reality and building a system to accommodate and profit from it, as was possibly the case at the Tower of Babel (Genesis 11). Christianity is the fact of the Creator Himself reaching into the created natural world and giving us by the Grace of the crucifixion and resurrection of Jesus Christ the fuller reality we need. The basic Truth of Christianity has been turned into a variety of religious expressions and systems that compete with each other. The saving Truth of Christianity can be received by anyone who is aware that they need God and that He can give them what they need for life and reality through the sacrifice of Jesus Christ. The Bible is vitally important to apply, establish in history and give necessary detail to this basic Truth. It should be treasured and studied by those to whom it is available.

Some great atheistic science fiction writers, like Stanislaw Lem, Phillip Pullman and Iain M. Banks, become aware of the Cloud and can be amazingly prophetic about the role of technology in our world.

Their books are often brilliant and engaging, although they tend to distort and parody the reality of the Cloud. Christians should not be disturbed by these books, but should read them to be aware of the cultural, intellectual and artistic world around us. We should not be afraid to love our neighbors in this way. Love requires us to care about what these writers and their readers think.

4

CAUTIONS

The Cloud is sometimes unsafe in various ways. Rebellious and destructive elements in the supernatural can present false revelations or temptations to people. Maybe we should call these "counterfeit cloud experiences". Genuine experiences are from God. We should stay awake and alert to examine our experiences of the supernatural and not only say "Like Wow!" or "Awesome!". Both genuine Cloud and counterfeit cloud experiences can be twisted by the agendas, fears and egos of people. People have individual, personal Cloud experiences that cannot really be shared. The Bible is the most comprehensive Cloud experience available to us. It can be shared, although some of

"Universal Man" from Hildegard von Bingen's Book of Divine Works (c. 1165)

our readings, misreadings and reactions to it cannot or should not be shared. The Bible serves us as a tool for evaluating Cloud experiences and life in general. The Cloud is the gate, interface or channel for visions, dreams, miracles, prophesies, inspirations, angel visits, healings, etc. These should all be tested for genuineness against the Bible.

It may be that some kinds of drugs, especially hallucinogenic drugs, can open a partial and distorted Cloud experience. In the 1960s sincere and courageous people believed drugs were a way into a fuller and more real life. Some died exploring this possibility. This hope soon faded into merely recreational use of drugs. Really effective musicians, filmmakers, poets, painters, novelists, singers, storytellers and others artists probably have more awareness of the Cloud than the average person. Their expressions and works cannot always be understood with the logic we usually use for the space-time part of reality. They have the power to expand our awareness, to help us see and know that reality is larger than we thought before. They help us experience relationships that logic will not show us. They are as necessary to human life and culture as scientists and craftspeople. However, these "artistic" people are all sinners and cannot be fully trusted to help us grow in a healthy way. All their works need to be tested.

Isaiah 44:22 reads, "I have swept away your offenses like a cloud, your sins like the morning mist. Return to me, for I have redeemed you." This biblical passage, among others, shows us that we can and do make a counterfeit cloud of our own, which is sin. The cloud of our own making does not open a gate and bring reality together. It separates us and encloses us in ourselves. If we identify with the cloud we make for ourselves, we will be blown away like a puff of smoke in the wind. This verse in Isaiah is particularly encouraging because it shows us that if we become poor in spirit, acknowledging our need of God and returning to Him through the Great Bridge Builder (Pontifex Maximus), Jesus, our counterfeit cloud is blown away but we are not. We are safe and solid in God's reality.

5

THE LORD'S PRAYER AND THE CLOUD

The prayer, plan and project of Jesus is for the Cloud event to become universal and permanent. He wants us to be with Him in this reality, so He gave us His Prayer. The prayer begins with "Our Father in Heaven". Heaven is the supernatural part of reality, not some place far away. Heaven is right here but we don't usually experience it.

Then comes the first request: "Hallowed be Thy Name" or May Your Name be known as Holy (on earth as it is in heaven). Holy means separate in Hebrew. God is separate from all that is counterfeit, false, rebellious or temporary. He is original, true and eternal. "Separate" does not mean partial or incomplete. Holy means "Wholly Real".

The next request is so important it is repeated. "Thy Kingdom come" and "Thy Will be done" mean the same thing. People have had various ideas about what the "Kingdom" means. Some have thought it means the Church. Some have thought it means some place far away. Jesus said various things about the Kingdom: He said it is coming. He said it is near. He said it is here. He said it is among you (in your relationships). He said it is inside you. Neither the Church nor someplace far away can be described in all these ways. The Kingdom of God is the Rule or Will of God. Jesus wants us to pray that the Kingdom will come here, permanently. He does not tell us to pray that we will be taken someplace else to be with God.

Jesus came, died, rose, ascended and will appear again to bind the natural and supernatural parts of reality together. He is the great healer and bridge builder.

The second half of the prayer about food, forgiveness and protection needs to be understood in the context of the first half, which sets the scene for these things.

6

PRAYER AND MEDITATION

We have mentioned prayer as an active way for people to engage in the Cloud connection. The words "prayer" and "meditation" are often used in a variety of ways. They are both vital parts of the Christian spiritual life and we must be careful not to be confused by the non-Biblical ways they are used. Perhaps we should start by saying that prayer should not be reduced to meditation, contemplation, thinking, imagining, feeling, action or work, silence, communion with nature, ecstatic or transcendental experience, although it does include some of these things. Nor is prayer union with the "ALL", ritual or magic. Prayer cannot be done or understood scientifically (mathematically). Prayer is not natural in the sense that it is not limited to the space and time parts of reality. It is not natural to people in the sense that it cannot be reduced to an evolved function of self-preservation or for the passing on of our genes. It is given by God as part of our full spiritual life. Prayer is personal in that it is a communication between one person and another Person. (Personal does not mean a consciousness that is aware of itself. Personal means self-aware consciousness in relationship with other self-aware consciousness.) Prayer is language – direct, definite and committed. If we read some of the prayers recorded in the Bible (e.g., I Kings 8, Col. 1:9-12, Eph. 1:15-29, Phil. 1:9-11), we find that God's people speak to Him in ordinary language about both this space and time existence and about the supernatural and eternity – the total reality in which we live our spiritual lives. God speaks to us through His Word (and His creation). We can speak to Him through our words about his Word and how it applies to our lives. We should take courage to pray and have communication with God, confessing our failure to make prayer the pervasive center of our lives. We can be truly centered in God and His reality by going beyond the center of ourselves and into the communicative relationship of prayer.

Meditation has a Biblical and non-Biblical meaning. In Psalms 49, 5, 19, 119, etc., the Hebrew word for meditation means, "to murmur, have a deep tone, sighing or moaning". We can think of Rom. 8: 22-27, which speaks of the creation "groaning" and the Spirit "groaning" for us. Biblical meditation is not a vague, transcendental experience or state of consciousness. The word appears most times in Psalm 119, which is one of the most highly organized chapters in the Bible. This structure suggests that meditation is not a disorganized, "going with the flow" kind of thing. Meditation is not disconnected from our reason and thinking about ordinary reality. Biblical meditation is not a process of unknowing but of knowing more fully.

Biblical meditation is about God's character or His actions. Thinking is a cerebral or mental activity that goes in a straight line. When we think, our minds move from A to B to C with an agenda to arrive somewhere at a conclusion. Meditation is more like taking some information about God (from the Bible or in agreement with the Bible) and holding it in our minds as if over a web or net so the Holy Spirit can show us places where it touches and applies to our lives that we never saw before. We might read something from the Bible about God, and in some way, hold it in our mind; or we might connect an experience with something in the Bible about God, which we hold in some way in our mind. Then we can think and pray about what He shows us. Meditation is more passive than thinking or praying; it is more allowing God to speak to us, while prayer is more us speaking to God. Thinking and meditation work together in a similar way that rational and emotional intelligence work together. They should not be in competition with each other. We should not choose one over the other. Much of life is like that. God made various contrasting things to belong together like the two sides of a coin: objectivity and subjectivity, left brain and right brain, unity and diversity, pre-destination and free will, mercy and justice, form and freedom, wave and particle, husband and wife, and others. The devil and our sinful natures are constantly tempting us to choose one side of the coin over the other. Some people may be naturally inclined to meditation, while others may be naturally inclined to prayer. God wants us to have both.

In the Eastern or New Age sense, meditation means to stop thinking and hold the mind completely still, raising ourselves up to a "higher" state of consciousness. This is very difficult to do and it does sometimes bring us into contact with the Cloud and the supernatural. It can have some therapeutic effects, which we enjoy. However, since we are not thinking, we cannot "test the spirits" as John commands us to do in I John 4:1-3, or "test everything" as Paul tells us in I Thessalonians 5:21. This kind of meditation is not so safe. It is also disobedient because we fragment the way God made and designed us to relate to Him, choosing one part over another. God is rational (and more than rational) and He has made us in His Image to be rational. When we come before Him to relate to Him, we must not deny or abandon anything except our sins. God sent Jesus to save us completely – our bodies, our minds, our spirits, our work, and our creative imaginations. We must present all of these parts of ourselves to Him as we grow in our spiritual life.

We should meditate about the deep things of the Lord, and we should think and pray before and after we meditate. Then we will avoid fragmentation and have a more full and safe relationship with Him.

7

THE SINGLE EYE

In Matthew 6:19-24 we read:

19. Do not store up for yourselves treasures on earth, where moth and rust destroy, and where thieves break in and steal. 20. But store up for yourselves treasures in heaven, where moth and rust do not destroy, and where thieves do not break in and steal. 21. For where your treasure is, thee your heart will be also. 22. The eye is the lamp of the body. If your eyes are good [SINGLE] your whole body will be full of light. 23. But if your eyes are bad [EVIL] your whole body will be full of darkness. If then the light within you is darkness, how great is that darkness! 24. No one can serve two masters. Either he will hate the one and love the other, or he will be devoted to the one and despise the other. You cannot serve both God and Money.

Here we have a section of three paragraphs in the Sermon on the Mount by Jesus. The first and third paragraphs are about a contrast and conflict between heaven and earth and God and money. The middle paragraph is a solution to the conflict or competition. In most modern translations, the "eyes" in verse 22 are described as "good", "sound", "whole", or "healthy", and the "eyes" in verse 23 are described as "bad", "unhealthy", or "unsound". But the original Greek words are "single" in verse 22 and "evil" in verse 23. We experience conflicts between investing in heaven or in earth and whether to serve God or money because we see reality as divided and the parts in competition. The Cloud revelation and experience allows us to have a single view of reality, held together by God. A divided view is evil because it is not God's intention that reality be divided.

Singleness of eye is related to singleness of heart. The eye is our view of reality, and the heart is our attitude to reality. When our eye and heart are single, we are integrated in ourselves and healthy. May God open the eyes of our hearts to see His original plan and saving healing.

8

SELECTED BIBLICAL CLOUD EVENTS

THE RAINBOW OF NOAH

In the account of the rainbow for Noah in Genesis 9, the Cloud is mentioned four times. Rain is not mentioned. There had recently been too much rain. The Hebrew word for rainbow is the same as for battle bow. The battle bow of God is not a natural phenomenon, in the same way that the hand of God is not a natural phenomenon. This shows us that the rainbow of Noah was not only a natural phenomenon but a manifestation of the interface or Cloud or bridge between heaven and earth, between the natural and supernatural parts of reality. The rainbow is a sign and reminder of God's Presence, His power to create reality and promise to sustain reality. Evil will never again be able to bring about so extensive a destruction as the flood. Perhaps we see the origin of this rainbow in Revelation 4:3, which refers to Jesus: "And the one who sat there had the appearance of jasper and carnelian. A rainbow, resembling an emerald, encircled the throne."

THE TABERNACLE

Much attention was given to detail in the construction of the tabernacle in the wilderness (Exodus chapters 24-31) because it would be the localized place of a continuing presence of the Shekinah Glory or Glory Cloud. Only the High Priest could enter the presence of the Shekinah Glory with the blood of the sacrifice. Eventually Jesus, the eternal High Priest, entered the heavenly dimensions with His Own Blood and the curtain separating the Shekinah Glory from all the people was torn from top to bottom. Now we enter into eternity and the presence of God the Father through the curtain of the body of Jesus, which was torn to make a gateway for us.

PENTECOST

The Pentecost event was another breaking through of the presence of God into space and time. Flame and wind are typical of the Cloud (no smoke or thunder in this case). Pentecost is a unique and permanent event of the presence of God with His people through the Holy Spirit. We read of a similar event in Numbers 11:24-25. "Moses went out and told the people what the Lord had said. He brought together seventy of their elders and had them stand around the Tent. Then the Lord came down in the Cloud and spoke with him, and He took of the Spirit that was on him and put the Spirit on the seventy elders. When the Spirit rested on them, they prophesied, but they did not do so again." In this passage "came down" does not mean to move from one place to another but to come from the supernatural dimensions into the natural dimensions. The two sets of dimensions are co-extensive and occupy the same place.

REVELATION

We see this movement in both directions in Revelation: "Look, He is coming with the clouds, and every eye will see him" (1:7) and "Come up here, and I will show you what must take place after this" (4:1). We see several elements of the Cloud in the following vision in Revelation 10:1-2:

"Then I saw another mighty angel coming down from heaven. He was robed in a cloud, with a rainbow above his head; his face was like the sun, and his legs were like fiery pillars".

THE CHARIOT OF EZEKIEL

Ezekiel (1:4) reports his experience of the Cloud like this: "I looked, and I saw a windstorm coming out of the north - an immense cloud with flashing lightning and surrounded by brilliant light." Then he saw in the cloud the chariot throne with wheels of interlocking wheels, turning without turning. These gyroscopes or stabilizers show us the dynamic stability of God, ever new and never changing.

THE BURNING BUSH

Moses (in Exodus 3) was confronted with the Cloud and experienced it as fire. It was localized at a bush but the bush did not burn up. The fire Moses experienced was not an oxidizing fire but the Shekinah Glory of Holiness. A voice came from the Cloud because the Cloud is a facilitator of various kinds of communication.

THE CHARIOT OF ELIJAH

Elisha (in 2 Kings 2) saw a "flaming chariot" when his teacher Elijah was taken into the supernatural dimensions in the Cloud. When the Aramean army surrounded Elisha, he could see the Cloud dimensions but his servant could not. Elisha prayed for the Lord to open his servant's eyes. Then the servant saw "the hills full of horses and chariots of fire all around Elisha."

THE DAMASCUS ROAD

The Apostle Paul (in Acts 9) experienced the Cloud on the road to Damascus. He saw flashing light and heard a voice. The experience blinded him for a while.

THE TRANSFIGURATION

The transfiguration of Jesus described in the Gospel of Matthew, chapter 17, is a clear and dramatic example of the Cloud. Peter, James and John saw Jesus transfigured with intense light. In the Cloud Jesus was with Moses, the Old Testament dead, and Elijah, the Old Testament undead. The disciples heard them talking about the only subject worth talking about—the death of Jesus that would bring victory and life to the whole world. Moses and Elijah had been saved by believing in the sacrificial death of Jesus and it had not happened yet in space-time history. The Cross is the center of history. People are saved by looking forward to it in history and believing God's

promises or looking back to it in history and believing God's promises.

JACOB'S LADDER

Jacob's dream (in Genesis 28) of the stairway in Genesis shows us that the Cloud is a two-way street with the angels or messengers of God moving both down and up. Jacob stopped in that place because the sun went down. It was a rather random choice but the place became special because of his experience. God can meet us in any place.

There are many other examples of this kind of thing in the Bible. Using these principles and examples you will be better able to understand the others that you come across.

Jacob's dream. Abilene, Texas. **Jack Maxwell**

THE STAR OF BETHLEHEM

If we can connect the Cloud with the Star of Bethlehem it can clear up some confusion and support the faith of some Christians. The Magi from Persia told Herod they had seen His star in the East. The star was not in the east. The Magi were. People called the cloud "light", "fire", "darkness" "chariot", "chariot throne". The Magi were Zoroastrians and astronomers. If they were confronted with the Cloud they would most naturally call it "star". A voice comes from the Cloud sometimes and gives information. This could have happened to the Magi. The Cloud could have "stopped over the place where the child was", while it is difficult to understand how a star could have done that.

Many have been confused and their faith challenged by the difficulty of understanding the Star of Bethlehem. If the

Magi were experiencing the Cloud of the Glory of God it might explain a lot and make the account more reasonable. Various calculations and charts have been devised concerning super nova and planetary conjunctions dated near to the birth of Jesus. These calculations might be correct, but they have two difficulties: the phenomena described could not have "stopped over the place where the child was" and the explanations are entirely naturalistic. The Cloud explanation includes miracle.

St. John Chrysostom added another element to this discussion in the 4th. Century in his 6th. homily on Matthew:

> *"...this star was not of the common sort, or rather not a star at all, as it seems at least to me, but some invisible power transformed into this appearance, is in the first place evident from its very course.*

For there is not, there is not any star that moves by this way, but whether it be the sun you mention, or the moon, or all the other stars, we see them going from east to west; but this was wafted from north to south; for so is Palestine situated with respect to Persia..."

Here is the text of the Star account from the Gospel of Matthew. Read it, substituting the word Cloud for Star and see if it makes sense. Matthew 2:1-10:

"After Jesus was born in Bethlehem in Judea, during the taime of King Herod, Magi from the east came to Jerusalem and asked "Where is the one who has been born king of the Jews? We saw his star [Cloud] in the east and have come to worship him." "When King Herod heard this he was disturbed, and all Jerusalem with him. When he had called together all the people's chief

priests and teachers of the law, he asked them where the Christ was to be born. "In Bethlehem in Judea," they replied, "for this is what the prophet has written: "But you, Bethlehem, in the land of Judah, Are by no means least among the rulers of Judah; For out of you will come a ruler Who will be the shepherd of my people Israel." Then Herod called the Magi secretly and found out from them the exact time the star [Cloud] had appeared. He sent them to Bethlehem and said, "Go and make a careful search for the child. As soon as you find him, report to me, so that I too may go and worship him." "After they had heard the king, they went on their way, and the star [Cloud] they had seen in the east went ahead of them until it stopped over the place where the child was. 10. When they saw the star [Cloud], they were overjoyed."

TWO CLOUD EVENTS THAT ARE OFTEN MISUNDERSTOOD

The Ascension and Second Appearing of Jesus are two important Cloud events that are quite often misunderstood.

Acts 1:9 describes the Ascension like this: "After he said this, he was taken up before their very eyes, and a Cloud hid him from their sight."

This Cloud is not water vapor but, again, the Shekinah Glory Cloud or what might be called the Cloud of Interface. Jesus was taken into the supernatural dimensions of reality so that He could not ordinarily be seen or heard in the natural dimensions. Jesus had earlier said two seemingly contradictory things which the Cloud helps us understand. He said, "I am going away" and "I am with you always". We can understand that Jesus is not in another place. He is in this place in other dimensions.

Many of the first generation of Christians believed that Jesus would appear again in total victory to establish His Kingdom during their lifetimes. Christians in Thessalonica were very upset and confused when some of them died and Jesus had not appeared. So, Paul wrote to reassure them in I Thessalonians 4:13-18:

13. Brothers, we do not want you to be ignorant about those who fall asleep, or to grieve like the rest of men, who have no hope. 14. We believe that Jesus died and rose again and so we believe that God will bring with Jesus those who have fallen asleep in him. 15. According to the Lord's own word, we tell you that we who are still alive, who are left till the coming of the Lord, will certainly not precede those who have fallen asleep. 16. For the Lord himself will come down from heaven, with a loud command, with the voice of the archangel and with the trumpet call of God, and the dead in Christ will rise first. 17. After that, we who are still alive and are left will be caught up together with them in the clouds to meet the Lord in the air. And so, we will be with the Lord forever. 18. Therefore encourage each other with these words.

Again, these "clouds" are not water vapor but the Shekinah Glory or interface. One of the most repeated ideas in the writing of Paul is that Jesus is King or Lord and Caesar is not. When Caesar visited a city, the elders came out to "meet" him and accompany him into the city. When Paul came to Italy from Malta and was travelling north to Rome, as we read in Acts

28:15, "The brothers there had heard that we were coming, and they traveled as far as the Forum of Appius and the Three Taverns to 'meet' us." They did not come to "meet" Paul to go back to Malta with him but to accompany him to Rome. So, when we (alive or dead) "meet" Jesus in the Cloud it is not to go with Him to someplace else but to accompany Him to the earth, where He is coming.

10

CONCLUSION

The vast majority of people all over the world and all through history, including today, have believed in some kind of supernatural reality that cannot be measured or understood using the tools we use to measure space-time reality. There have been many ways and systems to understand this other part of reality, some magical, some religious, some philosophical. Some of these ways have brought about a lot of confusion and suffering. The Bible is the best description for understanding the supernatural and how it interfaces with the natural. Both the natural and supernatural parts of reality were intended by God to function together as a whole. Because of rebellion, distortion and pride the parts of reality have been alienated from each other, resulting in various forms of death and suffering. God is sad and angry about this but He is not frustrated or defeated. He is succeeding in restoring reality to His Own perfect intention for it. The means of restoring and healing reality is Jesus. Through the world-making power of humility and sacrifice He has swallowed death up in victory and defeated the powers of darkness, death and alienation. The victory is sure and reality is moving surely towards a perfect healing.

The final permanent reality of a New Heavens and a New Earth cannot be perfectly understood in advance. In I Corinthians 2:9-10 Paul wrote:

> *"No eye has seen, no ear has heard,*
> *No mind has conceived What God has*

prepared for those who love him". But God has revealed it to us by his Spirit.

This passage means that what we know about the New Heavens and the New Earth cannot be fully expressed scientifically, rationalistically or philosophically. We know these things, as we know so many other things, by faith working in complementarity with sight.

All people suffer alienation and death within themselves and in their relationships with other people, with nature and with God. The power of the sacrifice of Jesus in the Crucifixion, which is healing the whole reality, is powerful to heal and restore individual people who choose to put their trust in Him. Consider the possibility that this is true very carefully.

The evil powers of alienation tell us we can have either the natural or the supernatural parts of reality. This is a terrible lie because Jesus died so that we can have both parts. Many people believe if they become aware of the Cloud they need to choose to abandon all their natural activities and concerns and begin to live transcendent lives rather than immanent lives. There is a fatal problem if we identify ourselves only in terms of the natural reality, but identification in terms of only the supernatural is equally fatal.

We can incorporate the knowledge and experience of the supernatural without abandoning the knowledge and experience of the natural. Keeping these two parts of reality together is like keeping both sides of the coin, or having a single view and attitude toward reality. The Biblical Cloud is the Cloud of knowing fully, not the Cloud of Unknowing. The Bible teaches us that true life is both transcendent and immanent – a total life in a total reality, provided and sustained by Jesus. Come to Jesus and have life.

The three crosses, **Rembrandt van Rijn** (1606-1669)

A POEM

When the material of this book was first given in lecture form at L'Abri Fellowship in Huemoz, Switzerland, Anna Friedrich, who is a worker at L'Abri, responded to it with this poem. It is printed here because sometimes the images and rhythms of a poem can help people understand something in ways that a prose paragraph cannot.

THE MATRIX OF TEA IS WATER

by Anna A. Friedrich

My face
comes close
to yours
-by that I mean
I see
bush and flame, barefoot
I see
pillars and pots
that flame, too, and move,
as if living.
I see
a hand that writes
on walls to warn-
a bright light, knocks me off my horse,
I'm hearing voices
(or thunder?)
I see you

breaking through, revealing
real needles
in all these smoking haystacks, but
I can only name the glow,
the haze,
the chariot,
a tongue, on heads?

Fumbling and veiled, I offer you
a tent
to make you permanent
-but you, dove-like, you ascend
radiant
and all I can say is
up and *clouds*.

35 QUESTIONS

As in the books "3 Theories of Everything" and "How Do You Know That?" the following questions were not written by the author. They were taken from recordings of actual Q&A sessions after lectures and from people who had read a draft of the text. The questions vary in style as well as content and are not polished. Some were spoken and some were written. They are included here partly to encourage you, the reader, to ask your own unpolished questions and engage with hope in the content of this book and life more broadly.

- **Is it possible to be open to the Cloud? If so, how?**

– Yes. The Bible gives us some instructions about this. It tells us to pray without ceasing, keep our eyes on Jesus and look to the Scripture as to a light in a dark place. Doing these things is not magic – it does not force God to do things for us and it is not a 1-1 cause and effect process. It does give us a vast and eternal perspective for our daily lives, which is realistic. It also keeps us aware of God and the blessings, comfort, strength and guidance that are available in Him.

- **Some Christians regard speaking in tongues as an embarrassment to the contemporary Church, as nowadays the phenomenon often seems to reflect not a spiritual gift but a kind of gibberish brought on by intense emotion, playacting, or self-deception. Have you ever met anybody who spoke in tongues, and where the tongue was one they did not previously**

know, and which was translated by somebody present who did speak the tongue?

– No. But that doesn't mean it doesn't happen. Apparently sane and honest people have reported witnessing such things to me, but only a few.

• New Age philosophy describes the "law of attraction" as a universal force which allows us to bring into our lives whatever we are focusing on. How does the law of attraction relate to the Cloud?

– In Philippians 4:8 Paul tells us, "Finally, brothers, whatever is true, whatever is noble, whatever is right, whatever is pure, whatever is lovely, whatever is admirable – if anything is excellent or praiseworthy – think about such things." We also need to think about the negative things in order to evaluate and avoid them. The things Paul wants us to think about are more real than other things. "Focusing" on these things keeps us open for God to "bring into our lives" what is real. Focusing on other things keeps us open for less real things to come in.

• **How do coincidences relate to the Cloud?**
– Some coincidences have an explanation, like meeting someone by surprise in an airport. Others not so much, like feeling a strong urge to make a phone call immediately, which turns out to prevent a suicide. The Cloud might facilitate this kind of awareness, which is more than rational, for Christians and non-Christians. The rain falls on the just and on the unjust.

• **How does quantum physics relate to the Cloud?**
– I am not a physicist nor a mathematician but some people who go deeply into these fields report experiences of beauty that cannot be expressed mathematically. Perhaps they are connecting with the Cloud in a similar way that artists, poets and musicians do.

- **Can the devil hear our thoughts?**
- Possibly. Knowing our thoughts would enable the devil to tempt us more effectively.

- **How does mind-reading relate to the Cloud?**
- In the Bible, there are several instances of God making people aware of what other people were thinking, possibly through the Cloud. It might be possible for gifted or sensitive people to access other people's thoughts through the Cloud but it is not a good idea. We should not develop techniques of mind-reading to further our own agendas but wait for God to show us these thoughts, if that his His will, to further His agenda.

- **Psalm 91 says that God "shall give His angels charge over you". Does this and perhaps other Biblical passages support the reality of guardian angels?**
- There is nothing in our lives that God does not care about. His messengers or angels are always

interacting or trying to interact with us. Sometimes this interaction can be directly obvious or even physical. We should be thankful. Folk religion and popular piety tell us some details about guardian angels which are not supported by the Bible. Matthew 18:10 records that Jesus said, "See that you do not look down on one of these little ones. For I tell you that their angels in heaven always see the face of my Father in heaven." "Angel" means "messenger". The messengers of little children's prayers see God. God hears us when we are very young. He probably hears us from the womb.

• **Is there something about the etymology of "religion" that shows us that Christianity is not a religion?**
— The medieval root of "religion" is "obligation, bond or reverence". The Latin root is "to bind" as in a ligament. Christianity is religious in our obedience and reverence to God. Many religions have

various systems of connecting to the supernatural. The basis of Christianity is not the system of responding but the fact of God connecting with us. The foundation of Christianity is what God does rather than what we do. It is easy to lose sight of this.

• You mentioned that in Revelation Jesus is coming with "clouds" plural. Could you expand on that?

– The Bible has many references to Clouds plural and to Cloud singular. Probably it is talking about the same thing.

• You connect that to Jesus' claim of being the gate to the door of the sheep?

– Jesus is the door, the gate and the way. Jesus is not the Cloud but the Cloud facilitates His being these other things for us. So, yes, there is a connection.

• **You said that the supernatural cannot be measured. Is it possible that we might be eventually be able to measure the supernatural scientifically, but just aren't there yet?**

– People can describe and measure more and more of reality with numbers as we move forward in history. Describing something with numbers is often a step toward controlling or producing it. I make a faith assumption that we will not be able to control or produce friendship, marriage or the Love of God, among other real things, beginning with describing them numerically. Some people make the opposite faith assumption. We need to think carefully about where our assumptions will lead us.

• **I wonder as Christians perhaps how we can open ourselves to the "unknowing" of the knowing?**

– If you mean something negative by "unknowing" of the knowing, we can open ourselves to this by concentrating strongly on one side of the coin or the other, which leads us to forget the neglected side. We can concentrate on the supernatural until we forget the natural or the other way around.

• You said reality is who God is, what he wants, and what he does. Could you give an example of this?
– God is Love, Light, and Spirit. These things and other attributes of God are real from the beginning through to the infinity/eternity of reality. God wants a creation and people in His Image to be creative in it. These things God sustains from the time they come into existence through to eternity. God does the creation and the saving of creation and remaking of creation. These things are eternally real. The details within these categories are infinite, of course.

- **Is there a danger in saying evil is not real? In saying that anything against God is not real? How would you deal with hell? Would you have to have an annihilationist view of hell?**

– If we believe that reality is Who God is, What He does and What He wants it opens the possibility of an annihilationist view but is not conclusive. The questions involved include: Does God want evil? Since evil is not an originally creative power will it be sustained by God for eternity? Is evil not as eternal as God in the past (evil had a beginning while God did not) but as eternal as God into the future? What does destruction mean? What does death mean?

- **Can we be deceived by the Cloud?**

– The Cloud is given by God as an interface of communication, which does not deceive us. If we manufacture our own "cloud" out of pride or ambition, then we will be deceived.

- **Early on you were criticizing the Gnostics. Do you not find sanctification a process of gnosis?**

– Gnosis means knowing, and sanctification involves knowing, of course. It also is growth that is more than gaining information or technique. It includes God giving us growth and identity in Christ. In sanctification we don't only know more and more but we are known and allow ourselves to be known.

- **So when the cloud moves away from the temple in Isaiah, is that a cutting off of the interface?**

– Basically yes. We can be thankful that the interface has been turned on again, especially through Jesus.

- **How was it in the beginning, in the garden of Eden?**

– Probably there was no need for the Cloud

because the people had direct access to God before they sinned. The Glory Cloud of God has always been real. When people became separated from God the Cloud took on newly needed connecting and relational functions.

• Is the church, as the community of the redeemed, the Cloud of interface now?

– No. The Church functions through the Cloud in relating to God in prayer, praise and intercession. We have new life and access to God through Christ only and live out that life in community with each other.

• Should the church prevent people from entering into the Cloud violently?

– It sounds like you are asking whether the Church should try to stop people from trying to force their way into the Cloud. In our Christian family communities, we should teach and encourage each other not to demand, claim or force connections with the Cloud according to our own imaginations or agendas—as in the case Nadab and Abihu mentioned earlier (Numbers 3:4). We should encourage poverty of spirit or knowing our need of God and being trusting and receptive as He gives us what we need.

• What actually happens when people try to force their way into the Cloud?

– The supernatural is not only benign. Just because an experience is supernatural doesn't mean that it is good. It is possible to force your way into contact with evil powers that will harm you. It is better to limit your involvement with the supernatural to your prayers to God and however He chooses to act into your life.

• **You said that people may develop techniques to achieve transcendence, and that this can be therapeutic. Can you say more about this?**

– We can use a variety of techniques, physical and mental, to help ourselves feel better. We can increase our general health through good breathing and posture; we can relieve stress and manage our anger through meditation. Mostly these things are not wrong but we should be careful not to confuse them with salvation and holiness, which are gifts of God rather than products of learned techniques.

• **Are "near-death experiences" cloud experiences?**

– It is very difficult, perhaps impossible, to analyze and evaluate these reported experiences, so I don't know. We should not expect to learn anything from these experiences that the Bible does not already teach us.

• **Can schizophrenia (and other mental disorders) be related to Cloud experiences?**
– Genuine Cloud experiences come from God and are not harmful. Possibly obsession or extended involvement with counterfeit "cloud" experiences can make us sick.

• **With what part do we connect to the Cloud or interface? Is it the heart?**
– The heart is not actually a part but the whole center of us, including the mind, body, will, strength, imagination. So, yes. It is the heart.

• **Is Jesus the interface?**
– Jesus is not the interface, but the way into the interface. Jesus is the veil, door or gate through which we enter into the Cloud interface and relationship with God.

• **Isn't the Holy Spirit the interface?**
– No, the Holy Spirit uses the interface in order

to relate to us. The Holy Spirit has been sent and works through the Cloud to bless, indwell, inspire, fill, guide, and rebuke us. The Holy Spirit and Jesus are persons with their own wills and agendas. They are not functions or phenomena that we use.

• Is music a way to interface?

– I hear you asking, Is music a way to connect with God? Music, both playing and listening to it, can be used to induce trance-like conditions that are pseudo-Cloud experiences. To do this is more than pleasure; it is usurping the prerogative of God in an effort to initiate a Cloud experience. It is not poverty of spirit, but pride. Sometimes music makes us more aware of the holistic nature of reality, which might be therapeutic in a good way. In this case our listening or playing is not an active attempt to open a gateway of communication with the supernatural, but rather experiencing an awareness of the Reality in a more passive way. As well as music, people can use drugs and various arts to produce for themselves sensations and experiences that get confused with Cloud experiences. We need to be careful about these things and not only follow what feels good.

- **Are there geographical places (or communities of people) that are "cloudier" – where cloud experiences are more likely?**

– There seem to be flow-lines of electric, magnetic and other energies that crisscross the earth and intersect at various points. On these points people have built religious and cultic structures. Some of the cathedrals of Europe have been built on the sites of ancient pagan temples. So it does seem that some geographical places are "cloudier" than others. Knowing this and visiting these places does not in itself bring us closer to God, but possibly into an awareness of the supernatural in general. We should not look to these places to bring us magical power.

– Communities of people have gathered at these sites for thousands of years. Communities of people anywhere which are devoted, rightly or wrongly, to contact with the supernatural, will tend to have more such contact. The Bible teaches us to pray together in communities. Sometimes people gather together in communities for witchcraft or other ways of grabbing power (e.g., getting rich or manipulating people in pride), which the Bible forbids.

• Is the subatomic world described by quantum physics closer to God than the world described by Newtonian physics?
– No, because both quantum and Newtonian aspects of reality are both created by God, and equally close to their Creator. In a similar way, neither objectivity nor subjectivity is closer to God than the other.

• **Paul instructed us to "pray without ceasing." Does this mean we are always praying using words? If we don't use words, how can we pray?**
– Maybe it will help to think again of working in a business with the Boss in the room. We are not always talking to Him but we are always aware that He is there and that we can talk to Him at any moment and be heard.

• **Can we still in some sense be prayerful even in situations when our minds are intensely absorbed in another mental task, such as calculating numbers, or reading a textbook?**
– Yes, if we develop the habit of mind of being aware that God is with us.

• **If a person goes through life and never experiences a Cloud event, does that mean that there is something wrong with their faith?**
– The ordinary things of life are those that give order and shape to life and are essential. Special

things are real and optional. Believing in God and His promises, trusting Him, obeying Him and speaking to Him are the ordinary things of faith. These things bring and sustain life for us whether we have special or dramatic experiences or not.

- **Do Christians experience more Cloud events than non-Christians?**

– Christians certainly experience prayer more than others but might not have more special experience than others. Special experiences don't save us. We are saved by knowing that we need God and trusting Him.

- **I had a powerful experience of God when I believed that Jesus is the Son of God. I've read about Satori – an experience that Zen Buddhism talks about. Are they the same thing?**

– A salvation experience and Satori have similarities but are profoundly different as well. They are both paradigm shifting and individual experiences. Both are an experience of an absolute and put peripheral considerations in perspective. Both should not become a memory but remain a present reality. However, an experience of Jesus is an experience of relationship and communication. Satori is an experience of unity and basic being. Satori gives a profound and universal experience of Self (Buddha nature). Salvation in Jesus gives us the full Image of God, which includes the self and goes beyond it. The basic nature of reality is relational rather than self-centered, so what we want and need is salvation in Jesus. My book 3 Theories of Everything goes into more detail on this question.

Copyright: Ellis Potter

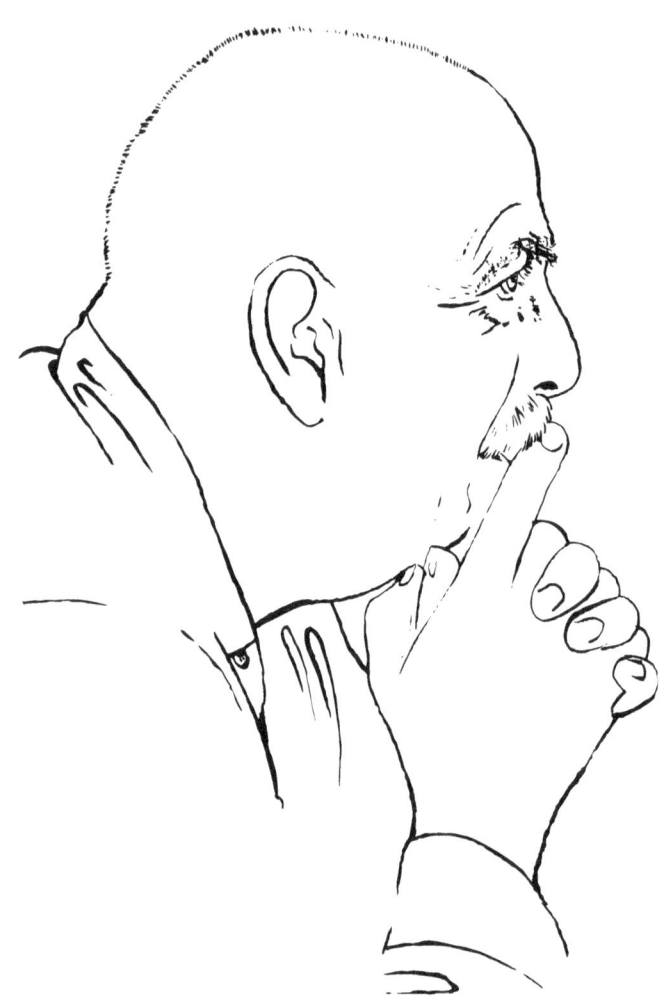

ABOUT THE AUTHOR

Born in California in 1948, Ellis Potter has resided in Switzerland since 1975. A former Zen Buddhist monk, he became a Christian in 1976 at L'Abri Fellowship under the influence of the late Dr. Francis Schaeffer.

After his conversion, Mr. Potter worked on the staff of L'Abri until 1991. He founded Eastern Europe Renewal in 1978 with his late wife, Mary, and has worked extensively in Central and Eastern Europe and all five continents.

Mr. Potter's unique background includes music, the arts, theology and philosophy. He lectures internationally on a variety of subjects, including comparing the Biblical and other worldviews, Spirituality, Art, Epistemology and Apologetics. His other books include: 3 *Theories of Everything*, *How Do You Know That?* and *Staggering Along With God – an interview biography*, all published by Destinée Media.

www.ingramcontent.com/pod-product-compliance
Lightning Source LLC
Chambersburg PA
CBHW071742080526
44588CB00013B/2125